SHORT WALKS TROSSACHS
CALLANDER AND ABERFOYLE

by Katie Featherstone

The Lower Woods Path near Callander (Walk 3)

CONTENTS

Using this guide..4
Route summary table 6
Map key 7
Introduction...9
  Walking around Callander, Aberfoyle and the Trossachs................10
  Things to see 10
  Where to stay..11
  Travel 11

The walks
1. Bracklinn Falls and Scout Pool............................13
2. Three Callander bridges 19
3. Callander Crags...25
4. East Callander circular....................................29
5. Falls of Leny 33
6. Loch Lubnaig and Strathyre Forest.........................39
7. Lendrick Hill and Glen Finglas 45
8. Loch Katrine and Primrose Hill 51
9. Creag Noran and Archray Water............................57
10. Ben A'an 61
11. Ben Venue...65
12. Doon Hill and Fairy Knowe 73
13. Lochan Spling 79
14. Little Fawn Waterfall and Lime Craig 83
15. Loch Ard and Lochan a' Ghleannain 89

Useful information...94

USING THIS GUIDE

Routes in this book

In this book you will find a selection of easy or moderate walks suitable for almost everyone, including casual walkers and families with children, or for when you only have a short time to fill. The routes have been carefully chosen to allow you to explore the area and its attractions. Most routes are circular or out-and-back, although some linear walks may be included that use public transport to get back to the start. Although there may be some climbs there is no challenging terrain, but do bear in mind that conditions can sometimes be wet or muddy underfoot. A route summary table is included on page 6 to help you choose the right walk.

Clothing and footwear

You won't need any special equipment to enjoy these walks. The weather in Britain can be changeable, so choose clothing suitable for the season and wear or carry a waterproof jacket. For footwear, comfortable walking boots or trainers with a good grip are best. A small rucksack for drinks, snacks and spare clothing is useful. See www.adventuresmart.uk.

Walk descriptions

At the beginning of each walk you'll find all the information you need:

- start/finish location, with a what3words address to help you find it
- parking and transport information, estimated walking time, total distance and climb
- details of public toilets available along the route and where you can get refreshments
- a summary of the key highlights of the walk and what you might see

Timings given are the time to complete the walk at a reasonable walking pace. Allow extra time for extended stops or if walking with children.

The route is described in clear, easy-to-follow directions, with each waypoint marked on an accompanying map extract. It's a good idea to read the whole of the route instructions before setting out, so that you know what to expect.

Maps, GPX files and what3words

Extracts from the OS® 1:25,000 map accompany each route. GPX files for all the walks in this book are available to download at www.cicerone.co.uk/1234/gpx.

What3words is a free smartphone app which identifies every 3m square of the globe with a unique three-word address, e.g. ///destiny.cafe.sonic. For more information see https://what3words.com/products/what3words-app.

USING THIS GUIDE

Walking with children

Even young children can be surprisingly strong walkers, but every family is different and you may need to adapt the timings given in this book to take that into account. Make sure you go at the pace of the slowest member and choose a walk with an exciting objective in mind, such as a cave, river, waterfall or picnic spot. Many of the walks can be shortened to suit – suggestions are included at the end of the route description.

Dogs

Sheep or cattle may be found grazing on a number of these walks. Keep dogs under control at all times so that they don't scare or disturb livestock or wildlife. Cattle, particularly cows with calves, may occasionally pose a risk to walkers with dogs. If you ever feel threatened by cattle, let go of your dog's lead and let it run free. Always bag and bin dog poo, or take it home.

Enjoying the countryside responsibly

Enjoy the countryside and treat it with respect to protect our natural environments. In Scotland, you can enjoy the outdoors on most land and inland water, as long as you act responsibly and follow the Scottish Outdoor Access Code – www.outdooraccess-scotland.scot.

The Scottish Outdoor Access Code

Responsible access can be enjoyed over most of Scotland including parks, hills, moors, mountains and woods, beaches and the coast, lochs, rivers and canals, and some areas of farmland. The key principles are:

Take responsibility for your own actions

- park sensibly and do not create an obstruction
- take your rubbish home

Respect the interests of other people

- respect the needs of other people enjoying or working in the outdoors
- follow any reasonable advice from land managers
- on farmland, leave gates as you find them and keep to unsown ground, field edges or paths
- access rights do not usually apply to farmyards, but if a well-used path goes through a farmyard, you can follow it
- paths are shared with others – let people know you are coming so you do not alarm them, and slow down, stop or stand aside if needed

Care for the environment

- don't disturb or damage wildlife or historic places
- never light open fires, barbecues or fire bowls in dry periods or near to forests, farmland, buildings or historic sites at any time
- never cut down or damage trees

ROUTE SUMMARY TABLE

WALK NAME	START POINT	TIME	DISTANCE
1. Bracklinn Falls and Scout Pool	Callander War Memorial	2½hr	8.5km (5¼ miles)
2. Three Callander bridges	Callander War Memorial	2¾hr	8km (5 miles)
3. Callander Crags	Callander War Memorial	2hr	6km (3¾ miles)
4. East Callander circular	Callander War Memorial	2¼hr	7.5km (4¾ miles)
5. Falls of Leny	Bochastle car park, near Kilmahog	1hr	4km (2½ miles)
6. Loch Lubnaig and Strathyre Forest	Ben Ledi car park north-west of Kilmahog	2½hr	7.5km (4¾ miles)
7. Lendrick Hill and Glen Finglas	Glen Finglas Visitor Centre near Brig o' Turk	2¾hr	8.5km (5¼ miles)
8. Loch Katrine and Primrose Hill	Trossachs Pier	3hr	11km (6¾ miles)
9. Creag Noran and Archray Water	Ben Venue car park	1hr	3km (1¾ miles)
10. Ben A'an	Ben A'an car park	2½hr	4km (2½ miles)
11. Ben Venue	Ben Venue car park	5–6hr	14.5km (9 miles)
12. Doon Hill and Fairy Knowe	Aberfoyle iCentre	2hr	6.5km (4 miles)
13. Lochan Spling	Aberfoyle iCentre	1¾hr	6km (3¾ miles)
14. Little Fawn Waterfall and Lime Craig	Aberfoyle iCentre	3hr	8km (5 miles)
15. Loch Ard and Lochan a' Ghleannain	Loch Ard Forest car park, near Aberfoyle	2½hr	7km (4¼ miles)

ROUTE SUMMARY TABLE

HIGHLIGHTS
Gorge, waterfalls, geology
Historic sites, rivers, views
Summit views, woodland
Historic sites, waterfall, woodland
Woodland, falls, river
Forest, views, loch
Ruins, woodland, reservoir, dam, waterfall
Loch, mountain views, woodland
Mountain views, woodland, river
Summit views
Summit views, forest
Fairy folklore, history, oak woods
Lochan, woodland, sculpture
Waterfalls, wildlife hide, forest, views
Loch and lochan, forest, sculptures

SYMBOLS USED ON ROUTE MAPS

- **S** Start point
- **F** Finish point
- **SF** Start and finish at the same place
- **4 ➤** Waypoint
- ～ Route line

MAPPING IS SHOWN AT A SCALE OF 1:25,000

0 KM   0.25   0.5
0 miles   0.25

DOWNLOAD THE GPX FILES FOR FREE AT
www.cicerone.co.uk/1234/gpx

Callander Crags above Callander (Walks 1–4)

INTRODUCTION

Ben A'an seen across Loch Achray (Walks 9 and 10)

Perched along the Highland Boundary Fault, the riverbank town of Callander and its smaller neighbour, Aberfoyle, provide the east and southern gateways to the world-famous, but surprisingly difficult to define Trossachs. At its most specific, the name 'Trossachs' refers to the region's leafy, green heart – a glen between the rocky peaks of Ben A'an and Ben Venue, with the outflow of Loch Katrine at its western border and Loch Achray to the east – but the term has grown to encompass a much larger area of forest, lochs and glens covering the central west of Loch Lomond and the Trossachs National Park.

Romantically known as Rob Roy Country, where folk hero Rob Roy MacGregor was born, ruled as clan chief and went on the run, this region of Scotland and the outlaw himself were brought into public imagination by the popular writing of early 19th-century poet and author, Sir Walter Scott. Four of his famous works relate to the Trossachs – *The Lady of the Lake*, *Waverley*, *Rob Roy* and *A Legend of Montrose* – using specifically named and identifiable places as settings for his fictional scenes.

Late Georgian-era visitors, captivated by Scott's evocative descriptions, were soon flocking towards Loch Katrine, earning the Trossachs its frequently used title 'the birthplace of Scottish tourism'. Belonging to the Highlands, but accessible from Glasgow, the area's popularity continued throughout Victorian times and endures to this day, inspiring a love of nature in successive generations.

In 2015 – 13 years after Loch Lomond and the Trossachs was designated as Scotland's first national park – a smaller area called The Great Trossachs Forest received additional status as a National Nature Reserve (NNR). Stretching between Callander and east Loch Lomond, the NNR has a 200-year plan, aiming to restore and diversify monoculture conifer plantations and heavily grazed hills; within the first 10 years more than 2.5 million native trees have been planted, creating and expanding varied habitat for the region's invaluable wildlife species.

Walking around Callander, Aberfoyle and the Trossachs

The walks in this book follow well-maintained paths, forest tracks and shared cycleways, many of which have reliable signage. Routes are predominantly circular, low to mid-level walks – any potentially difficult elements are explained in the walk introduction. Climbing to 729m, Ben Venue (Walk 11) is more of a challenge, intended for people who are feeling confident after comfortably completing some of the book's easier walks and are looking for something a bit longer with more elevation.

Walking in the Trossachs can be beautiful at any time of year, but there are substantial benefits of visiting in later spring, when there are more woodland flowers, or early autumn, when vast swathes of the forest are at their most colourful; waterfalls and rivers are always more impressive after rainfall.

Things to see

The Trossachs are famous for their expansive woodland, shimmering lochs and superlative hilltop views, but there are also tumbling waterfalls, intriguing historic sites and exciting wildlife species to discover – a glimpse of the orange flash of a native red squirrel is always a thrill, and look out for more elusive pine marten, osprey, golden eagle and black grouse.

The Trossachs is a red squirrel stronghold (Photo: Forestry and Land Scotland)

Craigmore above Aberfoyle (Walks 12–14)

Where to stay

Either Callander or Aberfoyle make a great base for accessing the walks in this book, with a range of B&Bs and a few hotels to choose from. Aberfoyle is slightly closer to the heart of the Trossachs, with three walks starting from the village and another one a short distance away; Callander is a bit further out, but also makes an excellent base, with four walks beginning directly from the town centre and another two nearby. In addition to these options, there are several private campsites and the camping permit areas run by the National Park Authority – the latter are dedicated places for wild camping, hidden within the forest, and the best option if you are looking to experience a little wilderness overnight. It is also perfectly possible to visit the Trossachs, Callander or Aberfoyle on a day trip from Glasgow.

Travel

It usually takes between 1½ and 2hr to reach either Callander or Aberfoyle from Glasgow on public transport. Callander is well connected by bus to Stirling, which is on the train line from Glasgow, and there's a direct bus from Glasgow to Aberfoyle. You can travel between Glasgow and Stirling by either bus or train. The national park authority's new, summer-only Trossachs Explorer bus aims to connect Callander and Aberfoyle with Loch Katrine and the majority of other walks in this book by running services every couple of hours during summer months. If you are driving, be aware that popular lochside car parks can be very busy during school summer holidays and bank holidays.

Unique rock formations at Bracklinn Falls

WALK 1
Bracklinn Falls and Scout Pool

Start/finish	Callander War Memorial, Ancaster Square
Locate	///remembers.purified.saves
Cafes/pubs	Plenty to choose from in Callander
Transport	Bus 59 from Stirling, 978 Scottish Citylink coaches between Edinburgh and Fort William
Parking	Bracklinn Falls car park (FK17 8EH), start walk from Waypoint 2
Toilets	Station Road, Callander

Time 2½hr
Distance 8.5km (5¼ miles)
Climb 240m

Steep in parts, this walk explores the Keltie Water, with a series of impressive gorges and falls

This rewarding circuit visits two dramatic sections of the Keltie Water river. The bridged Bracklinn Falls – an Anglicisation of the Gaelic name *A' Bhreac Linn*, meaning 'dappled pool' – has long been a popular spot for both local and visiting walkers due to its dramatic gorge and naturally sculpted rocks. From here, it's a steep walk upstream to Scout Pool and a second bridge over the river, rewarded by great views of the surrounding hills.

Looking towards Ben Vorlich from the northern bridge over Keltie Water

SHORT WALKS TROSSACHS

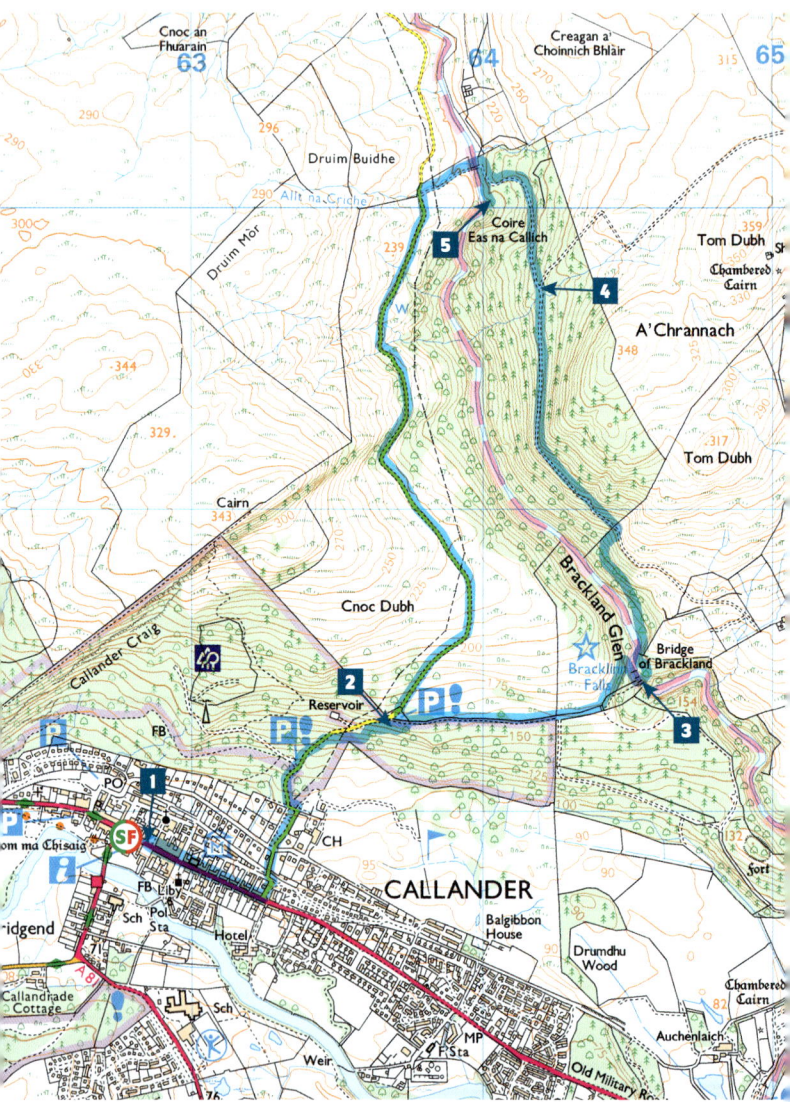

WALK 1 – BRACKLINN FALLS AND SCOUT POOL

Keltie Water tumbling down towards Scout Pool below

1 From **Callander War Memorial**, turn right onto Main Street and walk south-east for 430m, then turn left onto Bracklinn Road. Follow this for 900m to Callander Crags car park. From here, take the path indicated 'Bracklinn Falls 1 mile' on the opposite side of the road, which climbs gently through mixed woodland. As you approach Bracklinn Falls car park, a path bears right signed for Bracklinn Falls.

2 Follow the path east as it slopes gradually downhill. You'll hear the falls tumbling through the rocks below as you approach. Keep to the main path as it weaves down to the river – Keltie Water – and descend to **Bracklinn Bridge** (Bridge of Brackland) over Bracklinn Falls.

> ⓘ *The River Teith and its tributaries, including the Garbh Uisge and Eas Gobhain, are a Special Area of Conservation due to their importance to Atlantic salmon and three species of lamprey.*

> At the end of the last Ice Age, 17,000–12,000 years ago, large quantities of glacial meltwater cut the impressive gorge through which Bracklinn Falls tumble down.

3 Cross the bridge, which gives a dramatic perspective over the gorge below – here the river flows through the base of **Bracklinn (or Brackland) Glen** – then turn left, now following signs for 'Bracklinn Falls Circuit'. Follow the path, climbing steeply through deciduous woodland, before joining a forest track. Follow the track as it heads north-west and then north for 1km; it emerges from the forest approaching its high point, where it splits. Standing above Bracklinn Glen, you can see Ben Ledi and Ben Vorlich.

4 Take the left fork and follow the track downhill. As you reach a second bridge over a higher section of Keltie Water, don't cross it straight away, but turn left to leave the track onto a narrow, unmarked path beside the river. Follow the bank south for 200m to Scout Pool. Here, smooth, eroded rocks surround a calm pool in Keltie Water – a popular local swimming spot.

5 From Scout Pool, return to the bridge and cross it. Continue straight ahead for a short distance before turning left onto a minor road, signposted for Callander, and walk south for 2km back to the Bracklinn Falls car park. Retrace your steps along the path to Callander Crags car park, down Bracklinn Road and finally turn right onto Main Street to return to the war memorial.

A small waterfall flowing into Scout Pool

> ⓘ *Earth movements along the Highland Boundary Fault have twisted layers of rock from horizontal to almost vertical, something which can be seen at Bracklinn Falls.*

The Bracklinn Bridge

Bracklinn Bridge surrounded by mature oak trees

In 2004, a steel footbridge over Bracklinn Falls was washed away by severe floods. Because of its awkward location, it took six years for its striking replacement, a wood and copper construction, to be completed and hauled into place by hand. The new bridge won an award the following year, but by 2020 – less than a decade after its installation – it was deemed unsafe and closed. What you walk across today is the 21st century's third (and hopefully final) construction, which opened to the public in March 2023.

▬ To shorten
Walk as far as Bracklinn Falls (Waypoint 2) then retrace your steps to the start. This out-and-back walk is just over half the distance and less than half the elevation, and misses out the steepest and most difficult part of the main walk.

Looking towards Callander from the Samson's Stone path

WALK 2
Three Callander bridges

Start/finish	*Callander War Memorial, Ancaster Square*
Locate	*///remembers.purified.saves*
Cafes/pubs	*Plenty to choose from in Callander*
Transport	*Bus 59 from Stirling, 978 Scottish Citylink coaches between Edinburgh and Fort William*
Parking	*Meadows car park (FK17 8BA) or several other options in Callander*
Toilets	*Station Road, Callander*

Time 2¾hr
Distance 8km (5 miles)
Climb 210m

A varied, circular walk with excellent views following good paths to the south-west of Callander, taking in everything from history to nature

Following a lovely, meandering route through woodland and wide-open spaces, this predominantly low-level walk visits several historic sites, a conspicuous glacial erratic said to have been thrown by a giant, and the small summit of Dunmore Fort, which has expansive views over Loch Venachar and back to Callander town. There are good opportunities for spotting wildlife and bluebells are abundant in spring.

The red sandstone Callander Bridge over the River Teith

SHORT WALKS TROSSACHS

1 From **Callander War Memorial**, turn right onto Main Street for 120m, before turning right onto South Church Street. Pass the small Callander Community Friendship Garden and a restored sundial from 1753 and walk down to an old, metal-and-concrete bridge over the River Teith. From here there's a good view upstream to the red sandstone Callander Bridge. Cross the bridge, turn left (signposted for Coilhallan Wood) and follow a path, passing a rugby field on your right, down to the A81.

2 When you reach the road, turn right and follow the pavement for a short distance before crossing it and entering **Coilhallan Wood** between two stone pillars. Follow a path and signs west for 2km through mixed woodland and young birch trees to the edge of Coilhallan Woods car park. There are great views of Ben Ledi and Callander Crags.

3 Following signs for Dunmore Hillfort, turn left onto the road, walking through Easter Gartchonzie, then turn

WALK 2 – THREE CALLANDER BRIDGES

right to cross the arched **Gartchonzie Bridge** over Eas Gobhain. Follow the road 300m north-west to a T-junction. Cross the A821 here and join a path on its opposite side.

4 Continue straight on towards the wooded hill of **Dunmore Fort** until you reach a path junction, then turn left. After 200m, turn right onto a steeper, grassy path ascending the hill to its summit. There are fantastic views over Loch Venachar to the south-west and Callander in the east.

The remaining traces of Iron Age Dunmore Fort stand on a prominent puddingstone hillock. The harder rock here was more resistant to glacial erosion and was left, forming higher ground.

5 From Dunmore, continue on the path down the northern side of the hill. When you reach a path intersection in front of a drystone wall, turn right downhill and walk for 200m until you reach a second path junction. Here, turn left to cross a small wooden bridge and follow blue arrows along a grassy path up the south side of Bochastle Hill, passing through a gate, to the giant boulder, **Samson's Stone** near the summit. Continue past the rock along the path and follow blue arrows through young oak trees, silver birch and hawthorn back to a junction with the main path.

Samson's Stone is a metamorphic sandstone erratic, carried east by ice from the Highlands 12,000 years ago. According to legend, the giant Samson threw it from the top of Ben Ledi, proving himself to be champion of Scottish giants.

6 Turn left onto the main path and follow it north until you reach Bochastle car park. Here, follow signs to Callander, joining a path that runs

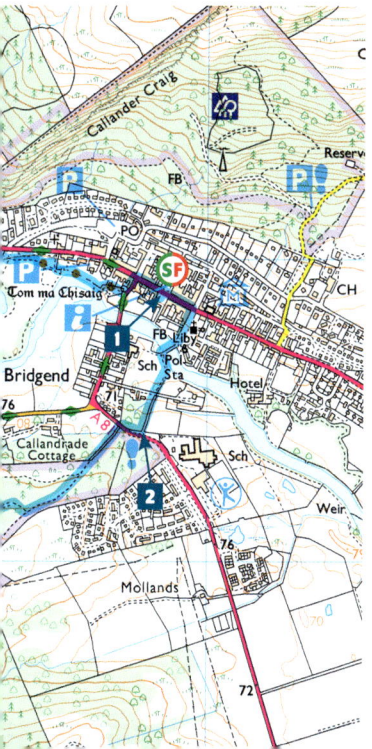

Loch Venachar from the summit of Dunmore Fort

> ⓘ *Native oak woodlands are an important habitat for redstarts, pied flycatchers and wood warblers, as well as other birds.*

beside the A821 for a short distance, then crossing the road to join a cycle path heading east. Follow the cycle path, which runs along the line of a dismantled railway, towards Callander as it passes the grass-covered remains of **Bochastle Roman Fort** on the left, then Little Leny Burial Ground – 200m down a side path through Little Leny Meadows – on the right.

Taking a break at Samson's Stone

WALK 2 – THREE CALLANDER BRIDGES

Bochastle Roman Fort, built about AD85, is an example of a 'glen blocker fort'. Located strategically to control exits from valleys leading out of the Highlands, they were used only briefly before being abandoned.

> ⓘ In the 1960s, Callander was known as the location for the original television series of Doctor Findlay's Casebook.

Continue along the cycle path to reach the walk's third and final bridge, a rusty metal construction.

7 Cross the bridge and after a further 130m, turn right onto a path (signed for Callander), which leads to Meadows car park, then walk along the bank of the River Teith to the peculiar, flat-topped lump of **Tom ma Chisaig** (Hill of Saint Kessog). This was probably a Medieval motte (castle mound) built to watch the bridge. Walk past Tom ma Chisaig and turn left onto Bridge Street, then take the first right onto Main Street and you'll soon be back at Ancaster Square.

– To shorten

To keep to easier ground and to avoid climbing Dunmore Fort and Bochastle Hill, walk to the path junction at the base of Dunmore Fort, then turn right onto the main path towards Bochastle car park, continuing the walk from Waypoint 6. This will save about 15min.

Little Leny Burial Ground in Little Leny Meadows

The Queens' Diamond Jubilee Cairn

WALK 3
Callander Crags

Start/finish	*Callander War Memorial, Ancaster Square*
Locate	*///remembers.purified.saves*
Cafes/pubs	*Plenty to choose from in Callander*
Transport	*Bus 59 from Stirling, 978 Scottish Citylink coaches between Edinburgh and Fort William*
Parking	*Callander Crags car park (FK17 8QE), start walk from Waypoint 2*
Toilets	*Station Road, Callander*

Time 2hr
Distance 6km (3¾ miles)
Climb 285m

A short, steep climb to a spectacular viewpoint, which looks over Callander, the Lowlands and hills to the north

While this route's steep, woodland ascent is a workout for the thighs, its clifftop summit – part of the Highland Boundary Fault – provides a dramatic perspective over Scotland's geological divide. The flat expanse of Callander and the Lowlands are spread out to the south-east, contrasting with the undulating hill country to the north. On a clear day, you can see Ben Ledi, Ben Vorlich and Stuc a' Chroin from here, as well as distant Ben Lomond beyond the Trossachs.

Looking north to the hills from Callander Crags

SHORT WALKS TROSSACHS

1 From **Callander War Memorial**, turn right onto Main Street and walk south-east for 430m, then turn left onto Bracklinn Road. Follow Bracklinn Road for 500m to Callander Crags car park.

2 Follow a forest track signed 'Callander Crags 2½ miles' through a barrier and walk down it for 200m, then turn right onto a narrower but obvious path that climbs steeply through woodland. When you reach the top, turn right (indicated 'summit') and follow a path along the edge of the crags for 200m to their highest point at the **Queens' Diamond Jubilee Cairn** at 343m.

> The conical stone cairn was built in 1897 and restored in 2000, now commemorating the diamond jubilees of both Queen Victoria and Queen Elizabeth II. It has spectacular views to Stirling and the Lowlands south-east, Loch Venachar and the Menteith Hills south-west, and the Highland peaks to the north and west.

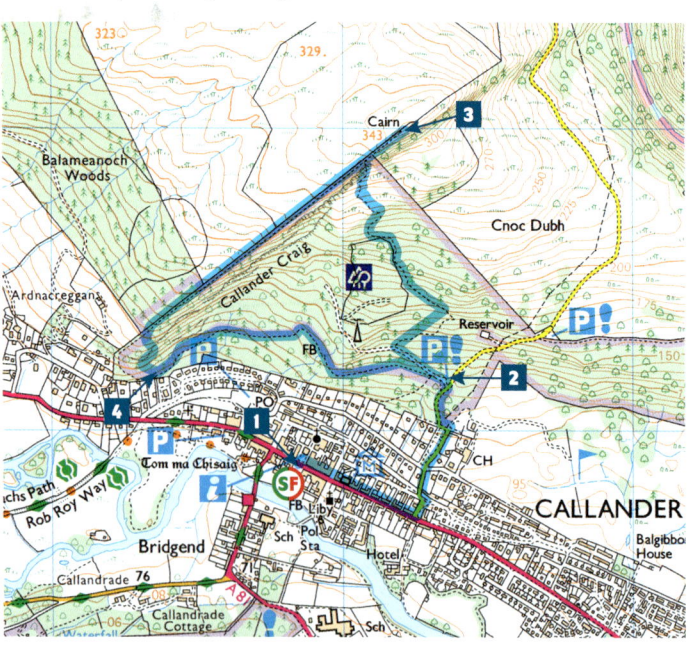

WALK 3 – CALLANDER CRAGS

The cairn was built in 1897 for Queen Victoria's Diamond Jubilee

3 Retrace your steps for 200m, then continue to follow the path along the top of the crags, **Callander Craig**, as it descends gradually south-west alongside a fence. The lumpy, exposed rock of the crags is puddingstone from the Devonian Period. Keep to the path as it winds back down into the woods, eventually bearing left and starting to level out on the approach to Callander.

4 As you come to the northern reaches of town, bear left onto the Lower Woods Path – initially marked with red waymarkers – then stay on the most obvious, main path as it rises, weaving its way east through mixed woodland. It climbs gently to a small viewpoint, before descending gradually towards Callander Crags car park. From the car park, rejoin the outward route, turning right to head back down Bracklinn Road, and right again onto Main Street towards Ancaster Square.

▬ To shorten

To save 1.5km and about 30min, once you've reached the bottom of Callander Crags at Waypoint 4, instead of taking the Lower Woods Path, turn right, following a sign for 'Town ¼ mile', and walk back into Callander via Tulipan Crescent and Leny Road, which lead onto Main Street.

Bracklinn Bridge over Bracklinn Falls

WALK 4
East Callander circular

Start/finish	Callander War Memorial, Ancaster Square
Locate	///remembers.purified.saves
Cafes/pubs	Plenty to choose from in Callander
Transport	Bus 59 from Stirling, 978 Scottish Citylink coaches between Edinburgh and Fort William
Parking	Meadows car park (FK17 8BAL) or several other options in Callander
Toilets	Station Road, Callander

Time 2¼hr
Distance 7.5km (4¾ miles)
Climb 125m

Following a shared cycle route and good paths, this walk visits a couple of interesting historic sites as well as Bracklinn Falls

Beginning along a straight section of disused railway, this ambling route covers ground shaped by glacial moraines, before passing two sites of prehistoric interest near Auchenlaich: a chambered cairn, thought to be the longest in Scotland, and an Iron Age hill fort. As you climb gently towards Bracklinn Glen, the peaceful mixed woodland – a good place for wildlife watching – shimmers purple with bluebells in spring, before descending to the dramatic gorge at Bracklinn Falls.

The ponds at Auchenlaich are popular with birds

SHORT WALKS TROSSACHS

1 From **Callander War Memorial**, turn right onto Main Street and walk south-east for 430m, then turn left onto Bracklinn Road. Take the first right, signed as a cycle path and for 'Bridge of Keltie 1½'. Follow cycle path signs east through the quiet residential streets of Murdiston Avenue and Livingstone Avenue. At the end of Livingstone Avenue, cross the road and join a shared cycle path, following a sign for 'Keltie Bridge'. Keep to this cycle path for 1km as it crosses Callander Terminal Moraine. The moraine is a bump running across the ground, left by an ice sheet's edge at the end of a cooling event around 12,000 years ago. Approaching **Auchenlaich**, where a few buildings stand beyond a picturesque duck pond ahead, you reach a path junction.

2 Turn left, following a sign for Bracklinn Falls. Head uphill, passing Auchenlaich Farm on your right and then a row of caravans (part of Keltie Bridge Campsite). Where a long, narrow field cuts between the caravans on your right, **Auchenlaich Chambered Cairn** runs under the track, stretching out to the north and south.

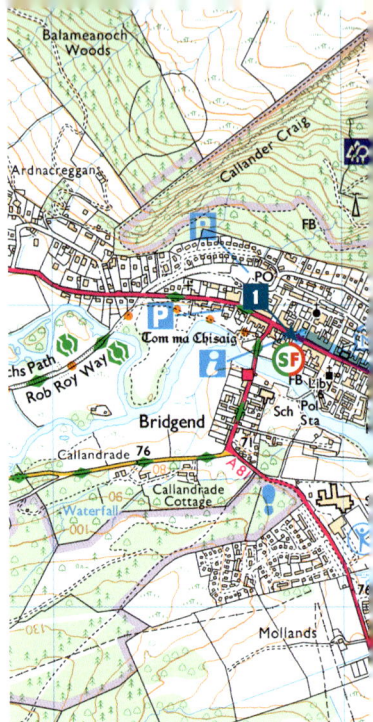

At 342m, Auchenlaich is Britain's longest chambered cairn. Thought to be 6000 years old, this Neolithic burial monument forms a noticeable ridge in the ground with some large protruding stones – these once formed part of the burial chambers.

Continue along the track for 200m, then take the sharp left turn up into mixed woodland for 400m to reach a track junction.

3 Bear right at the junction, following a sign for 'Bracklinn Falls ¾ mile'. A short distance after this, a post with an arrow indicates a side path to

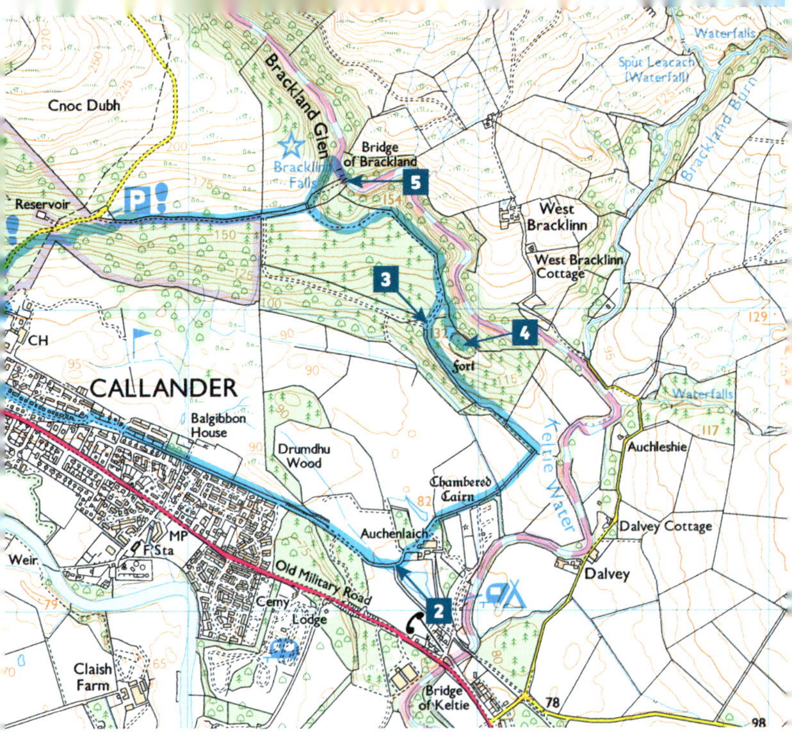

Auchenlaich Chambered Cairn

The woodland floor is thick with wildflowers, ferns and moss

Auchenlaich Hill Fort. Follow this for 200m through mature oak trees to the summit of a small hill, upon which once stood the fort.

> **Defended by a single rampart and external ditch, the 90m by 60m oval plan Iron Age hill fort is now somewhat lost in woodland, but would have held a commanding position in Bracklinn Glen.**

4 Once you're satisfied with your explorations, return to the main track and continue north uphill. Keep to the main path when the way is occasionally obstructed by fallen trees; it veers gently to the left and then right, eventually emerging from the trees. When the path splits at a junction, bear right (signposted for Bracklinn Falls) and follow the most substantial path as it weaves down to **Bracklinn Bridge** over the impressive gorge and falls.

5 Retrace your steps 250m uphill to the last junction and turn right, following a sign for 'Callander 1 mile'. Follow this path east for 1km, passing Bracklinn Falls car park on your right and continuing until you come out to Bracklinn Road opposite Callander Crags car park. Turn left onto the road and follow it back into Callander; when you reach Main Street turn right to return to the war memorial.

> **+ To lengthen**
>
> To extend the walk to Scout Pool, at Waypoint 5 join Walk 1 where it picks up at the Bracklinn Bridge (Walk 1, Waypoint 3) and follow it back to Callander. This would add about 4km, 110m ascent and about 2hr.

WALK 5
Falls of Leny

Time 1hr
Distance 4km (2½ miles)
Climb 35m

A short, gentle woodland walk to the powerful Falls of Leny

Start/finish	*Bochastle car park near Kilmahog*
Locate	*///digests.return.hologram*
Cafes/pubs	*Pub at Kilmahog (6min walk from start)*
Transport	*Trossachs Explorer (seasonal bus)*
Parking	*Bochastle car park (FK17 8HD) on A821 just south of river at Kilmahog*
Toilets	*No public toilets on route*

This relaxing woodland route follows a smooth, shared cycle path to a point where the Garbh Uisge tumbles over the Highland Boundary Fault, sculpting the riverbed rocks on its course between Loch Lubnaig and the mighty River Teith. The path down to the falls goes over uneven ground with exposed tree roots to an unfenced viewpoint above the high bank. The return route then weaves along the riverbank, between trees, keeping to a narrow, trodden path through the verdant woodland floor. Look out for leaping salmon in autumn and the small birds that thrive amongst Scotland's native broadleaved trees.

The shared cycle path runs along a disused railway line

Mature oak trees line the path

WALK 5 – FALLS OF LENY

1 From the car park, follow the cycle path indicated 'Falls of Leny 1¼ miles' – this begins by heading north a short distance beside the A821 road. When you reach a junction, turn left onto National Cycle Route 7, which heads north-west in an elevated position above the **Garbh Uisge**, taking an initially straight line along the course of a disused railway. This was once the route of the Callander to Oban train line. Continue along the cycle path through deciduous woodland for 1.7km until you reach a concrete bench and an information board about migrating salmon.

2 Turn right, leaving the cycle path behind to join a trodden path heading for the riverbank. Between October and mid-November, it's possible to spot Atlantic salmon leaping over rocks in the river on their journey upstream to spawn. After a short distance, a steep, narrow path heads off to the left – taking care of the uneven

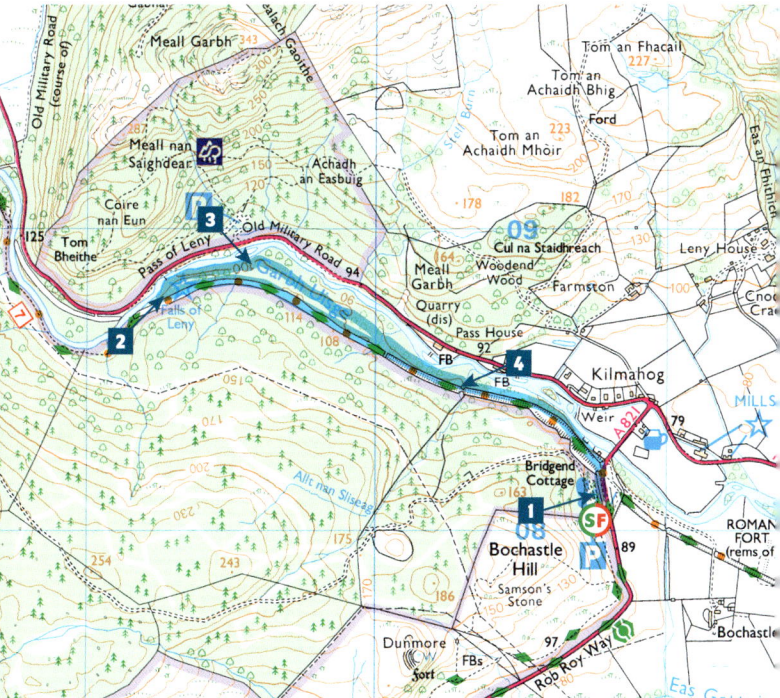

SHORT WALKS TROSSACHS

> ⓘ *The Highland Boundary Fault was formed by the collision of two continents 390 million years ago. This remarkable rocky ledge stretches right across Scotland.*

ground, exposed tree roots and the precipitous riverbank, follow this to get a closer look at the **Falls of Leny**. Continue east beyond the falls with the Garbh Uisge below on your left, following a network of snaking paths that run along the raised riverbank for 300m.

Here, sandstones, slate and schist formed as sediments in an ocean that existed in the southern hemisphere 600–400 million years ago,

Greater stitchwort thrives in shaded woodland habitat

Falls of Leny

before being buried and metamorphosed under enormous pressure by the same mountain-building process that closed the ocean.

3 At the junction here, avoid the narrow path that descends to a lower level beside the water – this eventually runs out – and instead keep to a mid-level path between oak trees, which

leaves the riverbank behind. When you reach a stone bridge over a small burn on your right and two sturdy metal fence posts, turn right and follow a path up to the cycle route.

4 Turn left onto the cycle path and retrace your outward steps for 500m back to the road. Finally, turn right to return to the car park.

> **– To shorten**
> **Returning along the smooth-surfaced cycle path makes this route a little shorter, and also wheelchair or bicycle accessible.**

Several burns flow down into Loch Lubnaig along the return route

WALK 6
Loch Lubnaig and Strathyre Forest

Time 2½hr
Distance 7.5km (4¾ miles)
Climb 215m

Following forest tracks at the foot of Ben Ledi, this straightforward walk has great views over Loch Lubnaig

Start/finish	Ben Ledi car park north-west of Kilmahog
Locate	///lived.lessening.diner
Cafes/pubs	Cafe at Strathyre Cabins
Transport	No public transport
Parking	Ben Ledi car park (FK17 8HD) off A84 (initially signed 'Strathyre Cabins' from road, cross bridge, then turn immediately left for car park)
Toilets	No public toilets on route

On this uncomplicated route, the initial 200m climb up the south-eastern flank of Ben Ledi is quickly rewarded by excellent views of Loch Lubnaig and the hills on its eastern bank. After descending through the layers of mixed woodland that make up the southern reaches of Strathyre Forest, the return route follows the bank of Loch Lubnaig along a section of the Rob Roy Way.

The bulk of Ben Ledi rises above the forest

WALK 6 – LOCH LUBNAIG AND STRATHYRE FOREST

Looking down on Loch Lubnaig

1 From Ben Ledi car park, walk north 150m to the west side of the road bridge over **Garbh Uisge** (if you arrived by car, this is the way you came in). Bear left and walk across the small car park here onto a path leading uphill, north-west, signed 'Ben Ledi'. Follow the path as it climbs steeply with a first view of Loch Lubnaig and the hills beyond to reach a junction.

> As you climb you pass Callander Commemorative Grove, where native trees have been planted by school children in memory of the 67 soldiers listed on Callander War Memorial.

2 At the junction, turn right and follow the forest road for 400m and then, when it splits, take the left fork onto a track heading uphill – follow this around a bend. On a clear day, the tower of Stirling's Wallace Monument can be seen in the distance south-east.

3 Continue straight ahead on the most obvious, main track through this southern part of Strathyre Forest for 3km, ignoring an intersecting gravel track, a turning marked for Ben Ledi

> ⓘ *Loch Lomond and the Trossachs National Park was established in 2002, followed by the Cairngorms National Park the next year.*

Loch Lubnaig narrows as it runs into the Garbh Uisge

and another track leading uphill on your left at Meall Dubh. Eventually, the track comes to a sharp right turn as it avoids a wooded hillock called **Tom Bheithe**; keep following the track as it descends to **Loch Lubnaig**.

The bulk of Ben Ledi ('hill of the slope' in Gaelic) dominates the view west, while looking down over the forest and Loch Lubnaig, the hills beyond include Beinn Bhreac ('speckled mountain') and Beinn Each ('mountain of horses').

− To shorten

A largely level, wheelchair or bicycle accessible route follows a shared access road along the Rob Roy Way beside Loch Lubnaig. From the start at Ben Ledi car park, head north directly to Waypoint 4 on the map. The return route is 1hr or 3.5km, or further if you want to continue.

+ To lengthen

Turn left when you reach the loch at Waypoint 4 and walk as far as you like along the Rob Roy Way, which continues north along the entire length of Loch Lubnaig. Retrace your steps to continue the main route.

WALK 6 – LOCH LUBNAIG AND STRATHYRE FOREST

4 On reaching the loch, turn right at the junction – forming part of the Rob Roy Way, this shared access lochside road continues for just over 2.5km back to the start of the walk, passing Strathyre Cabins where there is a cafe. Various side-paths allow you to pop down to the shore of the loch. Look out for dippers – small, bobbing birds at the water's edge.

> ⓘ *Loch Lomond and the Trossachs National Park covers 1870 square km^2 with 22 lochs.*

Rob Roy MacGregor

Bluebells line the lochside in spring

Born by Loch Katrine, Rob Roy (1671–1734) was the third son of cattle dealers Donald Glas MacGregor of Glengyle and Margaret Campbell. Chief of the controversial MacGregor Clan, Donald Glas was a Jacobite – part of a political movement supporting the restoration of James VII to the throne. Age 18, Rob Roy fought beside his father in the Battle of Killiecrankie, later going on to become a cattle drover, clan chief, outlaw and then fugitive. He lived near Loch Lomond until he died in Balquhidder (at the northern end of Strathyre Forest) aged 63.

Glen Finglas Reservoir and Toman Dubh

WALK 7
Lendrick Hill and Glen Finglas

Start/finish	*Glen Finglas Visitor Centre 600m east of Brig o' Turk*
Locate	*///segregate.cabin.anyone*
Cafes/pubs	*Tea room and pub at Brig o' Turk*
Transport	*Trossachs Explorer (seasonal bus) to Brig o' Turk*
Parking	*Glen Finglas Visitor Centre (FK17 8HR) off A821*
Toilets	*At visitor centre*

Time 2¾hr
Distance 8.5km (5¼ miles)
Climb 235m

This route follows good paths and woodland tracks, visiting a couple of pretty waterfalls, with great views over the glen

The setting for both an early poem by Sir Walter Scott and a famous portrait of the art critic John Ruskin, this wooded glen between mountains has been capturing artistic imagination for centuries. Today, the area is run by the Woodland Trust, who provide a series of waymarked walking trails and information boards to help you explore. A number of viewpoints from Lendrick Hill look over Glen Finglas forest and the surrounding hills, including a great view of Ben Venue.

Walking through woodland on Lendrick Hill

SHORT WALKS TROSSACHS

46

WALK 7 – LENDRICK HILL AND GLEN FINGLAS

Drippan ruined farmstead

1 From Glen Finglas Visitor Centre, walk downhill through the car park (with the road on your right), then turn left to follow an orange arrow marked 'north', passing a wooden information sign to cross a bridge. Follow a substantial path through a large wooden gate – when it splits shortly afterwards, continue straight on. The path climbs through mature oak trees to Drippan ruined farmstead, indicated by a sign, slightly off the path to the right. The remains of these stone walls would have been part of a farming township 200 years ago. Return to the path and continue uphill for 250m to a junction.

2 Turn left, following a sign for 'The Glens'. After 100m, a waymarked side path on the left will take you to a slender **waterfall** which plummets over high rocks amongst the trees. From here, return to the main path and continue, crossing a bridge after a short distance. Follow the path as it rises through the trees, emerging at a series of viewpoints from Lendrick Hill, one with a bench. Continue to follow the path as it descends, passing through a gate in a deer fence to reach a junction marked with three boulders.

3 Turn left (signed 'Brig o' Turk') onto a quiet, private road and follow it as it descends through mixed woodland for just under 1.5km. Along the way, there are several clearings in the trees, where you can look over **Glen Finglas Reservoir**, the dam at its south end

Glen Finglas Reservoir dam

and the tiny island of Toman Dubh. Pass through a gate and go past an information sign to Dam Road car park.

> Glen Finglas is an Anglicisation of the Gaelic, Gleann Fionnghlais, meaning 'glen of the white stream'. The Rev. James Stewart, who worked with poet Dugald Buchanan to translate the New Testament into Gaelic, was born here in 1701.

4 At the car park, turn right (leaving the orange waymarked route behind for a detour). Go through a gate to follow the private Glen Finglas Road above the tumbling **River Turk** on your left. After 500m, when you reach a clearing with a bench, a sign for 'waterfall' indicates a side path to Ruskin Viewpoint. Return to the private road and continue over a bridge towards the **dam** above. When the road splits, take the lower, right fork to get a view of the impressive dam from below, then climb the steps on your left for a shortcut to the left-hand fork, which continues up around a corner to the top of the dam. There's a great view across Glen Finglas Reservoir from here.

5 Return to Dam Road car park and continue walking down the road between two 20mph road signs, picking up the orange waymarkers once

WALK 7 – LENDRICK HILL AND GLEN FINGLAS

again and passing a few houses on your right. After 400m, look out for a turning onto a gravel path through a kissing gate on your left, signposted for 'Visitor Gateway'.

6 Follow this path as it rises through woodland before emerging through another kissing gate onto a well-trodden path through a grassy clearing. Going back into the trees briefly, look out for an orange arrow pointing left at a junction and join a raised, wooden walkway that goes over **Brig o' Turk** mires. Reaching a gate, go through it, turn left and go through another gate, continuing along a wooden walkway and then a path beside the road, which leads you back to the visitor centre and car park.

> The mires used to be used as a curling pond when they froze over in winter. They are now preserved for plant and wildlife – look out for dragonflies and smaller damselflies flitting amongst the wildflowers.

Brig o' Turk mires

− To shorten

Leaving out Ruskin Viewpoint and the dam makes this walk 1km and 30min shorter. When you reach Dam Road car park (Waypoint 4), turn left and continue the instructions from Waypoint 5.

✛ To lengthen

At Waypoint 3, turn right onto the private road and walk north alongside and above Glen Finglas Reservoir for more great viewpoints. When you've had enough, turn around, retrace your steps and continue along the road to Dam Road car park to complete the route.

Ruskin Viewpoint

Ruskin Viewpoint

Ruskin Viewpoint, where the River Turk spills over rocks through a gorge, was the setting for a famous portrait of the leading Victorian philosopher and art critic John Ruskin, painted by his protégé John Everett Millais in 1853. When, in 1965, the dam was introduced upstream, the painting's location was thought to have been lost but was rediscovered several decades later. It's said that while working on this portrait, Millais fell in love with Ruskin's wife, Effie. Ruskin and Effie's seven-year marriage was annulled in 1854 on the grounds of never having been consummated. A year later Millais and Effie married.

WALK 8
Loch Katrine and Primrose Hill

Start/finish	Trossachs Pier by Loch Katrine Visitor Centre
Locate	///ghosts.swarm.player
Cafes/pubs	Cafes and food vendors around the car park
Transport	Trossachs Explorer (seasonal bus) to visitor centre
Parking	Trossachs Pier car park (FK17 8HZ)
Toilets	At the car park

Time 3hr
Distance 11km (6¾ miles)
Climb 255m

A longer, but simple walk with a long climb to a great vantage point over Loch Katrine, returning beside the shore

Propelled to fame by Sir Walter Scott's 1810 poem *The Lady of the Lake*, picturesque Loch Katrine has been an enduringly popular visitor destination since late Georgian and Victorian times; Queen Victoria herself enjoyed a boat trip here. This walk begins at the loch's eastern end – the very heart of the Trossachs – following a shared tarmac track just above the loch shore, before making a woodland ascent of Primrose Hill to a series of spectacular viewpoints.

Looking out over Loch Katrine

SHORT WALKS TROSSACHS

1 Walk to the far end of the car park, towards and past Pier 2, and continue along the shared tarmac track, with the loch on your left. Walk past Loch Katrine Eco Lodges, and around the track's first bend is a small waterfall where **Allt na Cailliche** flows into the loch. Continuing for 300m, crossing a bridge over a series of weirs at Glen Finglas Works.

> Loch Katrine has been the primary water reservoir for much of Glasgow and its surrounding areas since 1859. Additional water from nearby Glen Finglas Reservoir is moved to Loch Katrine by a tunnel, which flows out here.

2 Walk past the headland of **Am Priosan** on your left, coming to a view out to two tiny, wooded islets and the larger **Eilean Molach** or Ellen's Isle. Continue along the track and, 350m past Eilean Molach, look out for a right

Glen Finglas Works

Walking along the Primrose Hill path

turn indicated 'Primrose Hill Trail' with a wooden sign and green waymarkers.

3 Take this steep, stoney path uphill and follow it as it climbs 65m over the first 500m. Continue along the path as it rises more gradually through mixed woodland with ferns and heather undergrowth. On reaching a track junction, bear right to follow a green marker uphill. Eventually, just as you begin think the hill is never-ending, a clear view over **Loch Katrine** appears as you approach the path's high point above Brenachoile Lodge and its pier. On a clear day, you can see the Arrochar Alps on the far side of Loch Lomond – look out for The Cobbler's obvious horn.

4 Keep following the path, which starts to descend in zigzags, with a view of Ben Venue and the islands near Trossachs Pier. Go through a

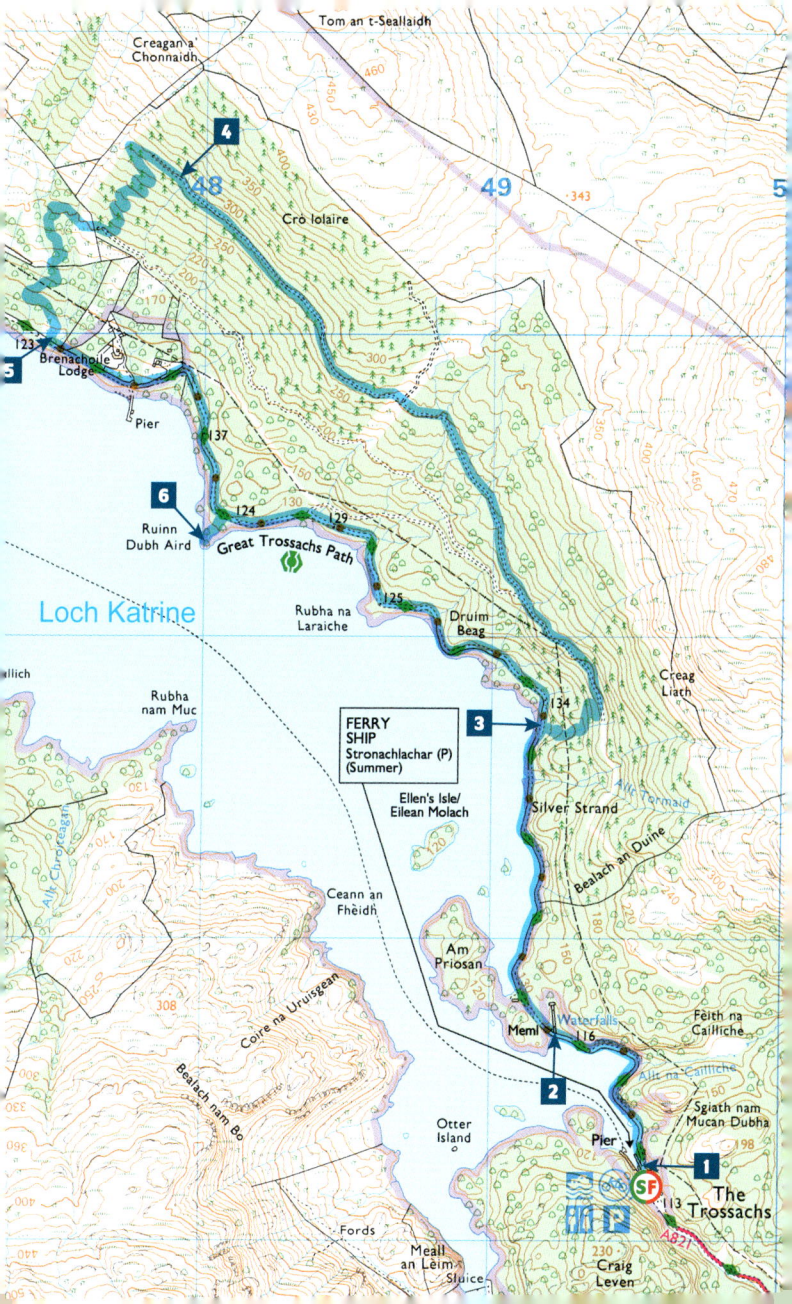

kissing gate and cross stepping stones over a stream as the path rises a little before descending again through oak trees. When you reach the junction with the paved, lochside track, turn left following a sign for 'Trossachs Pier'.

> ⓘ *Red squirrels are threatened by squirrel pox, a disease carried by non-native grey squirrels. So far, very few greys have managed to migrate to the Highlands.*

5 Walk along with Loch Katrine now on your right. Pass between **Brenachoile Lodge** and the small pier and boathouse, then continue for 700m to **Ruinn Dubh Aird** or Brenachoile Point. Indicated by a sign, this low headland stretching into the loch is an ideal spot for a picnic.

6 When you've finished enjoying the view, return to the shoreside track and continue 3.5km back to Trossachs Pier.

Taking in the view at Brenachoile Point

Visitors enjoying a boat trip on the loch

– To shorten
The shared, tarmac lochside track is flat and accessible for people with reduced mobility, wheelchair users and bicycles. A 1hr 45min, 7km out-and-back route visits Brenachoile Point, but going any distance will give good views of Loch Katrine.

+ To lengthen
At Waypoint 5, turn right instead of left and walk west as far as you like before returning to continue the route.

Eilean Molach or Ellen's Isle

Ellen Douglas was Sir Walter Scott's *Lady of the Lake*, the woman for whose affections three men were fighting. This small island in Loch Katrine – which was larger before the water level in the loch was increased to supply Glasgow – features in the poem as the residence of Ellen and her family. Historically speaking, the island was a stronghold of Rob Roy's Clan MacGregor and is said to have been a hideaway for fugitives. While the words 'Eilean' and 'Ellen' might look similar, *eilean* is Gaelic for 'island'; Eilean Molach means 'shaggy island'.

Ben A'an seen over the leafy Trossachs from Creag Noran

WALK 9
Creag Noran and Archray Water

Start/finish	Ben Venue car park
Locate	///depend.blemishes.stew
Cafes/pubs	None on route
Transport	Trossachs Explorer (seasonal bus)
Parking	Ben Venue car park (FK17 8HZ)
Toilets	No public toilets on route

Time 1hr
Distance 3km (1¾ miles)
Climb 65m

This winning wee walk starts and ends with great views, ambling along the riverbank for its midsection

Combining the waymarked Creag Noran trail with a gentle wander along the Achray Water riverbank, this short but rewarding route has wonderful views of the leafy Trossachs, over beautiful Loch Achray and to the distinctive peaks of Ben A'an and Ben Venue. Despite being no great distance from the main road, the walk feels surprisingly secluded, peaceful and wild.

The lovely Loch Achray from Creag Noran

1 Two paths leave from the back of Ben Venue car park; take the one on the right indicated 'Ben Venue and Creag Noran Viewpoint Trail', which climbs uphill. Follow the path for 360m to a viewpoint at **Creag Noran**. From these craggy rocks there are glorious views of Ben A'an to the north, Ben Venue west and Loch Achray in the east. Continue along the path for 130m until you reach a junction.

2 Following a sign for 'Ben Venue Hill Path', turn right and head downhill, with a great view of Ben Venue ahead. Keep to the path as it continues onto a wooden walkway, which ends at a road junction with a small car park. Turn left (indicated for Ben Venue) and walk down a private road, passing pretty, white metal gates and a sign for Loch Katrine Dam. Follow the road alongside **Achray Water** for 550m until you reach a left turn onto a path signposted for Ben Venue. Take this path and walk down to a charming, **arched footbridge**, which serves as an excellent viewing platform for the torrents of Achray Water spilling over rocks. This stretch of river connects Loch Katrine with Loch Achray.

The footbridge over Achray Water

Bracket fungus on the bank of Achray Water

3 From the bridge, turn around and retrace your steps along the path and then private road to the small car park at the road junction. Here, take the first right, following a sign for 'Car Park' and join the wooden walkway once again. Follow the path as it ascends to the path junction. Now, turn right, following a sign for the car park and blue waymarkers. There are more great views of Ben A'an as you descend for 400m back to the car park.

> **– To shorten**
> Simply follow the blue waymarkers of the Creag Noran Viewpoint Trail for a route of roughly 1km.

Heading towards the pointed summit of Ben A'an

WALK 10
Ben A'an

Start/finish	Ben A'an car park
Locate	///firelight.joked.incisions
Cafes/pubs	None on route
Transport	Trossachs Explorer (seasonal bus)
Parking	Ben A'an car park (FK17 8HY)
Toilets	No public toilets on route

Time 2½hr
Distance 4km (2½ miles)
Climb 330m

The short but very steep ascent of a well-maintained path to a spectacular view from the summit of Ben A'an

A miniature mountain, Ben A'an's rocky, conical summit rising from the forest is one of the Trossachs' most striking sights. The only thing to beat looking *at* it, is to look out *from* it – those who brave the steep, rocky ascent are rewarded with unbeatable views over Loch Katrine, Loch Achray and Loch Venachar, as well as of the nearby Ben Venue and surrounding mountains.

A family enjoying the view from the summit of Ben A'an

SHORT WALKS TROSSACHS

1 From the car park cross the A821 and go through wooden posts onto an uphill track with a sign for Ben A'an. This soon becomes a well-built path, as it ascends steeply (at one point splitting briefly before rejoining), then crosses the **Allt Inneil** by a footbridge. Continue as the path levels with Ben A'an looming directly ahead, looking to be the preserve of rock climbers from this angle (it isn't!).

Walker on the Allt Inneil footbridge

WALK 10 – BEN A'AN

We can blame Sir Walter Scott for the Anglicisation, 'Ben A'an'. The hill's proper Gaelic name was Am Binnean meaning, appropriately, 'the pinnacle'.

Some 500m after the bridge, the path crosses a forest track.

2 Ignore this crossing track and carry on straight, soon entering birch trees. Continue for another 400m to a clearing with large boulders. With a view of Ben Venue, this makes a good spot for a picnic.

3 From the clearing, follow the path as it ascends steeply up a series of rock steps beside a stream, then splits into vague branches to cross it. Keep going as it levels out, running to the right of the summit cone (ignore the eroded short-cuts on your left). The path circles round to a col before bearing left for the final ascent of the rocky summit of **Ben A'an** (454m).

From the top, serpentine Loch Katrine snakes out west, while Ben Venue dominates the south-west; to the south-east Loch Achray and its larger neighbour Loch Venachar stretch towards Callander. On a clear day, you can see as far as the Arrochar Alps.

4 From the summit, simply retrace your steps to the car park – just remember to go straight ahead when the path reaches the crossroads with a forest track.

Walkers descending the path towards Loch Achray

The path runs along beside Gleann Riabhach

WALK 11
Ben Venue

Time 5–6hr
Distance 14.5km (9 miles)
Climb 675m

Start/finish	*Ben Venue car park*
Locate	*///depend.blemishes.stew*
Cafes/pubs	*None on route*
Transport	*Trossachs Explorer (seasonal bus)*
Parking	*Ben Venue car park (FK17 8HZ)*
Toilets	*No public toilets on route*

A real challenge route and the longest climb, with rocky ground and unmarked paths leading to incredible views

With some boggy areas and rocky ground, as well as a 675m ascent, this walk is definitely a challenge, but Ben Venue's spectacular, panoramic views make the effort worthwhile. From the summit, you can see most of the national park's peaks, as well as looking down over Loch Katrine and the dense tree cover of The Great Trossachs Forest. A more serious endeavour than other walks in this guidebook, Ben Venue should only be attempted if the weather forecast is good. Wear sturdy footwear and make sure you take some warm and waterproof clothing, just in case.

A broken trig point at the south-eastern summit with Loch Achray and Loch Venachar beyond

SHORT WALKS TROSSACHS

1 The first 3km of this route, as far as the end of Waypoint 4, are well sign-posted for Ben Venue. From the back of Ben Venue car park, take the path on the right, which climbs uphill past the viewpoint at **Creag Noran**. Follow it for nearly 500m until you reach a junction. Here, turn right and walk downhill. The bulk of Ben Venue looms over the trees up ahead. Keep to the path as it joins a wooden walkway, then follow it to a road junction with a small car park.

2 At the junction, turn left and walk down a private road, passing white gates and a sign for Loch Katrine Dam. Follow the road alongside a river for 550m until you reach a signposted left turn. Take this path and walk down to an arched footbridge over the tumbling **Achray Water**. Continue straight

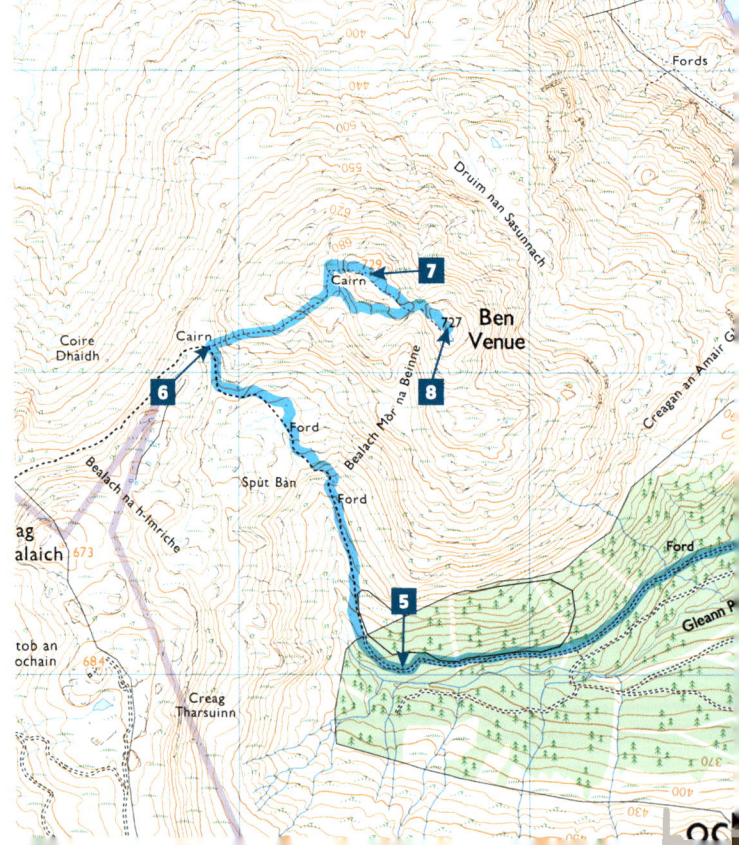

WALK 11 – BEN VENUE

along a track for a short distance, then turn right onto another track. Follow this track west for 350m, looking out for a 'Ben Venue' sign pointing left.

3 Take this turning, following a wide path as it rises between tall trees. Look out for red squirrels here. After 450m, ignore a left turn at a junction and continue uphill for another 250m. When you reach a T-junction with a forest track, turn left onto it and walk for 160m. As the track begins to bend left towards a bridge, turn right onto a narrower path, signed for Ben Venue, which soon crosses a burn. Follow this path for 240m as it emerges from the mature forest to an area of young trees to reach a junction with a track.

4 Cross the track and continue walking uphill on a good path. The

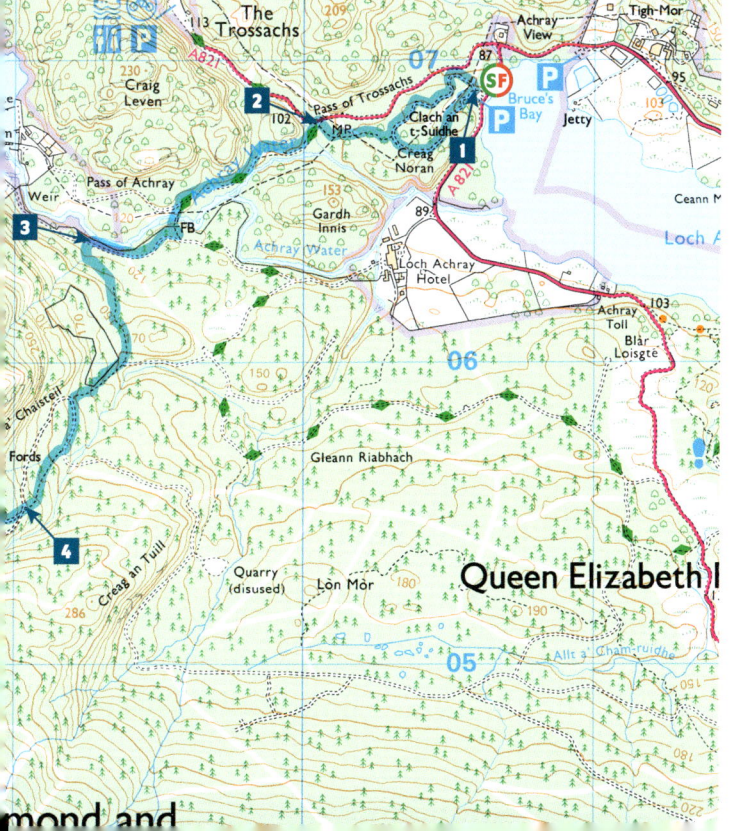

The path heads to the right of Spùt Bàn waterfall

signposts end here, but follow this path as it heads roughly south-west above the valley **Gleann Riabhach** for just over 1.5km – Ben Venue is now on your right and you will be following the course of Gleann Riabhach for most of the ascent. Ben Venue is A' Bheinn Mheanbh in Gaelic, meaning 'the small mountain', though it might not feel like that on your way up!

5 Keep to the well-made path as it begins to bear right and climb north towards and past a slender waterfall called **Spùt Bàn**. The path becomes less distinct as it climbs above and to the right of the waterfall with some exposed rock to cross. After 150m, as the path dips into a wet, grassy col, look out for a continuation of the path on your left beyond a boggy area; rather than heading directly for the path, make a wide, anticlockwise semicircle around to it, crossing two small burns and avoiding the worst of the bog. Rejoining the path, keep to the most obvious strand as it splits, climbing for a further 300m, and emerge to a rocky **cairn** and junction at 580m elevation.

6 Turn right, following a steep, rocky path east-northeast for 450m. When the path splits just before descending steeply, with the highest point you can see directly ahead, turn

> ⓘ *In Gaelic Loch Achray is Loch Àth Chrathaidh, meaning 'loch of the ford of shaking'.*

WALK 11 – BEN VENUE

left onto a narrower path, which will take you to the true summit of **Ben Venue**. Follow it alongside a few rusty fence posts before climbing steeply (past more fence posts) to the summit cairn at 729m.

> Loch Lomond and the Trossachs National Park is spread out around you, with countless mountain peaks north and west, and Loch Katrine below. From the south-east summit, there are also great views over Loch Achray and Loch Venachar towards Callander.

7 Walk past the summit cairn and walk south-east along a path which descends a little, heading towards a second, slightly lower summit. After 200m this path meets the larger bypass path – bear left onto this and clamber up its final section, over some exposed rock, to a broken trig point at 727m.

8 To descend, retrace your steps for 200m, then keep to the bypass path, contouring round to the left of the true summit. Follow it down to the rocky cairn at 580m, then turn left, following

> ⓘ *The name Loch Venachar comes from the Gaelic Loch Bheannchair, meaning 'horn-shaped loch'.*

Looking towards the Cobbler from Ben Venue

A walker and her dog at the true summit

your outward route as it runs down the rocky valley, then follows the course of Gleann Riabhach back to the forest.

Follow well-placed signs for the car park back through the forest to the start of the walk.

– To shorten

Emerging from the trees at Waypoint 4, there are good views south. If the walk turns out to be more of a challenge than expected, or if the weather isn't looking good, turn back here, cutting the route down to 6km and about 2hr.

Climbing Doon Hill through oak trees

WALK 12
Doon Hill and Fairy Knowe

Start/finish	Aberfoyle iCentre
Locate	///vies.learns.bless
Cafes/pubs	Plenty in Aberfoyle
Transport	X10A bus from Glasgow or Stirling
Parking	Aberfoyle Riverside car park (FK8 3UQ)
Toilets	Next to Aberfoyle iCentre

Time 2hr
Distance 6.5km (4 miles)
Climb 125m

Swathed in fairy folklore, this route follows good paths through native oak trees

Entwined with the story of Robert Kirk, a 17th-century, fairy-obsessed reverend, this meandering walk ties together history with folklore and the natural with the supernatural. A varied circuit, it crosses the River Forth twice, climbs the 77m Doon Hill, where people still leave offerings for the fairies, and wanders through a north-eastern part of Loch Ard Forest, dense with oak trees, healthy moss and bluebells in spring.

The Minister's Pine

SHORT WALKS TROSSACHS

1 From Aberfoyle iCentre, turn right and walk towards Riverside car park. Go across the car park, turn right and walk towards a bridge. Cross this bridge over the **River Forth** and continue straight along the road heading south-southwest, passing the few houses that make up **Kirkton**. After 440m, the ruined Kirkton Church and its burial ground are on your left. Built in 1744, the church was built on the site of an older building where Robert Kirk served as minister.

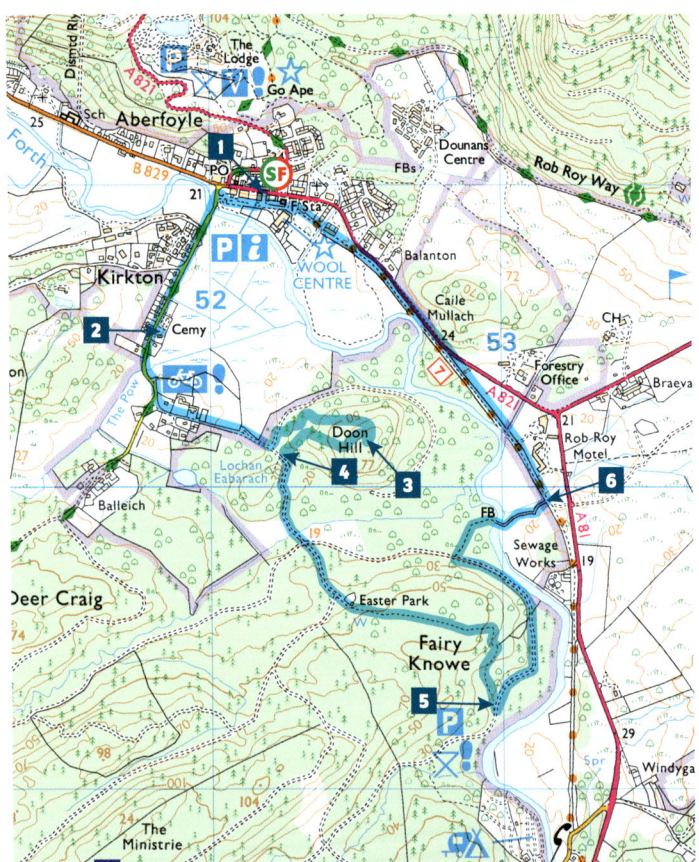

The heavy iron coffins outside the ruined Kirkton Church

Two iron coffins by the entrance are mortsafes, used to protect corpses from early 19th-century body-snatchers. Around the back of the church is Robert Kirk's gravestone, with a carving of a thistle above a crossed sword and pastoral staff.

2 From the church, continue along the road and cross a bridge; 100m further, turn left onto a minor road, with a sign for 'Doon Hill Trail'. Follow this road through a few houses as it disintegrates to track and passes through a barrier. Some 20m beyond the barrier, turn left onto a smaller gravel path, then, after another 40m, turn right onto a path that leads uphill. Follow the path through mature oak trees, looking out for wooden carvings of mushrooms and other fairy-related sculptures along the route, to climb **Doon Hill**.

3 On the summit plateau, a singular Scots pine tree standing in a clearing amongst the oaks is known as the **Minister's Pine**, decorated with all manner of offerings to the fairies. It is sometimes said that Robert Kirk's spirit is trapped inside a fairyland within the tree. To descend, retrace your steps across the clearing and, some 20m from the tree, find a path with a green marker to the left of your ascent path. Follow this downhill until you reach a T-junction, then turn left onto a track.

SHORT WALKS TROSSACHS

Tributes to the fairies are dotted along the path up Doon Hill

4 Walk along the track for 300m, cross a small bridge and go straight ahead at a track crossroads. Continue for another 230m until the track takes a sharp right turn, forming a second crossroads with two paths – here, go straight ahead, where there is a blue marker beside a path heading uphill. Follow this path over a slight hill in the woodland called **Fairy Knowe** until you reach a junction with a track after 860m. These native oak trees support a rich ecosystem, with mosses, ferns and wildflowers carpeting the woodland floor, creating habitat for insects, birds and other wildlife.

5 Turn left onto the track and follow it for 720m, ignoring a blue waymarked path on your right, until you reach a junction signed for Aberfoyle. Take the right turn here and cross an arched bridge over the River Forth. Bear slightly left and follow a path north-east across a field until you reach a junction with a cycle path.

6 Turn left onto the cycle path and follow it back to **Aberfoyle**, where it comes out by Aberfoyle Riverside car park and Aberfoyle iCentre (on your right).

WALK 12 – DOON HILL AND FAIRY KNOWE

− To shorten

A shorter route of 3.5km and 1hr 15min visits Doon Hill without Fairy Knowe, following green waymarkers; at Waypoint 4, turn right onto the track (instead of left) and within 100m, you will reach the barrier mentioned in Waypoint 2, from which you can retrace your steps back past Kirkton to Aberfoyle.

+ To lengthen

To add 400m and 15min, at Waypoint 6 walk along the cycle path for 800m, then turn left to follow a path along the bank of the River Forth back to Aberfoyle – the meadows here are rich with plants and wildlife, including kingfishers.

Reverend Robert Kirk

One of the most influential characters in the history of Scottish magical tradition, Reverend Robert Kirk (1644–1692) was a Gaelic scholar, folklorist and author of *The Secret Commonwealth of Elves, Fauns and Fairies*, written in 1691. As minister of Kirkton Church from 1685 until the year he died, he is said to have learned the information for his book from his parishioners. In 1692, Robert Kirk dropped dead while on a walk. The story goes that he was taken by the fairies as a punishment for revealing their secrets and remains trapped in fairyland to this day.

Carvings on Robert Kirk's gravestone

A sculpture in Lochan Spling made by the artist Rob Mulholland

WALK 13
Lochan Spling

Start/finish	Aberfoyle iCentre
Locate	///vies.learns.bless
Cafes/pubs	Plenty in Aberfoyle
Transport	X10A bus from Glasgow or Stirling
Parking	Aberfoyle Riverside car park (FK8 3UQ)
Toilets	Next to Aberfoyle iCentre

Time 1¾hr
Distance 6km (3¾ miles)
Climb 75m

An easy walk following tarmac and gravel tracks to a pretty lochan

This gentle and straightforward route takes the old Statute Labour Road from Kirkton to little Lochan Spling in Loch Ard Forest. Peaceful, mixed woodland around the lochan shore provides valuable wildlife habitat – look out for dragonflies and damselflies flitting over the water. The tarmac and firm gravel tracks make the route accessible for a wide range of people; taking bicycles would be another option.

Looking out from the viewpoint at the far east of Lochan Spling

SHORT WALKS TROSSACHS

1 From Aberfoyle iCentre, turn right and walk towards Riverside car park. Go across the car park, turn right and walk towards a bridge. Cross the bridge and continue straight along the road heading into **Kirkton**. The striking small hill above Aberfoyle on your right is called Craigmore. Take the third right turn (signed 'Statute Road'), passing a postbox and a few houses as the road turns to stoney track. Continue straight on, following the Statute Labour Road for just over 1km as it heads through the mixed woodland of north-east Loch Ard Forest to reach a crossroads.

The Statute Labour Road connects Aberfoyle with Stronachlachar. It was originally intended to service the Inversnaid Garrison, which was built on the land of Rob Roy's MacGregor Clan in 1718 following the Jacobite uprising of 1715.

2 At the crossroads, go straight on (signposted 'Statute Labour Road and Loch Ard') passing a 'No unauthorised vehicles' sign. Soon, you can see the first glimpses of Lochan Spling through the trees on your right, but don't worry, there are better views on the other side. Continue for 1km, past

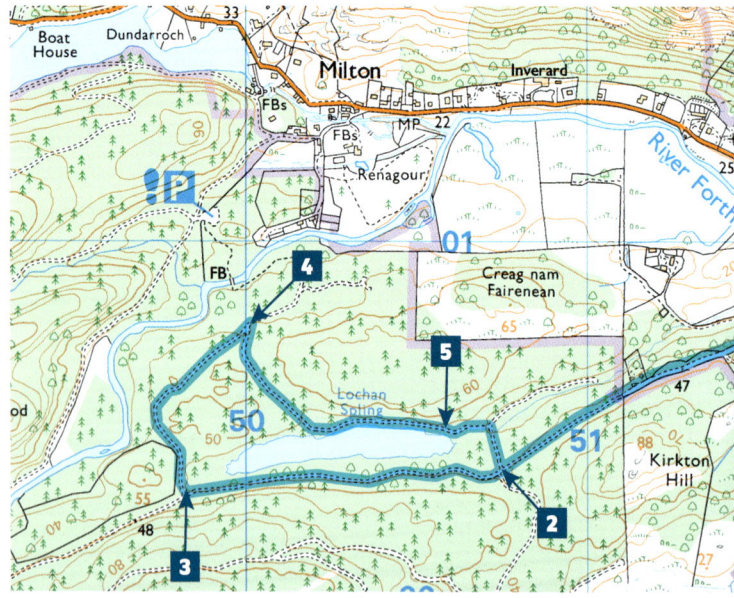

Following the Statute Labour Road

the far west end of the lochan, until you reach a junction.

3 Turn right, following a sign for 'Lochan Spling Trail, Statute Labour Road Loch Ard'. Keep to the main trail for 650m, soon heading north-east with good views of **Craigmore** up ahead. When you reach a junction with a bench, turn sharp right.

4 Follow the path uphill into tall conifers over a rise and down to the shore of the lochan. A metal dragonfly sculpture hovers above the water's surface. Continue along the path, heading east along the northern shore of **Lochan Spling**. At the lochan's far east end, there is a viewpoint with a bench and good views towards the hills further west.

The mixed woodland around Lochan Spling creates a variety of habitats for insects and wildlife

5 To return to **Aberfoyle**, continue along the path as it leaves the lochan behind, following a little stream then crossing it at a junction – keep to the main path as it bears right here. Some 130m further on, pass a barrier gate to reach a crossroads, then turn left following a sign for Aberfoyle. Retrace your outward steps along the Statute Labour Road, turn left at Kirkton, then walk back over the bridge and through Aberfoyle Riverside car park to the walk's start.

− To shorten

For a walk of 4km and about 1hr, turn right at Waypoint 2, walk past the barrier gate and follow the main path for 250m as it bears around to the left to a viewpoint at the east end of Lochan Spling. From here, retrace your steps to Aberfoyle.

WALK 14
Little Fawn Waterfall and Lime Craig

Time 3hr
Distance 8km (5 miles)
Climb 310m

A long climb along waymarked forest tracks with two waterfalls, red squirrels and a great viewpoint

Start/finish	Aberfoyle iCentre
Locate	///vies.learns.bless
Cafes/pubs	Cafe at The Lodge
Transport	X10A bus from Glasgow or Stirling to the iCentre, Trossachs Explorer (seasonal bus) to The Lodge
Parking	The Lodge (FK8 3SX), start from Waypoint 2
Toilets	Next to Aberfoyle iCentre and at The Lodge

Firstly visiting The Lodge, run by Forestry and Land Scotland, this longer walk winds its way along well-made forest tracks and paths. The route visits the attractive Little Fawn Waterfall and a wildlife hide frequented by red squirrels, before climbing to the edge of the Highland Boundary Fault and emerging above the treeline to great views. Start the route from The Lodge to miss out the first steep section.

The steep path up to the viewpoint above Lime Craig

SHORT WALKS TROSSACHS

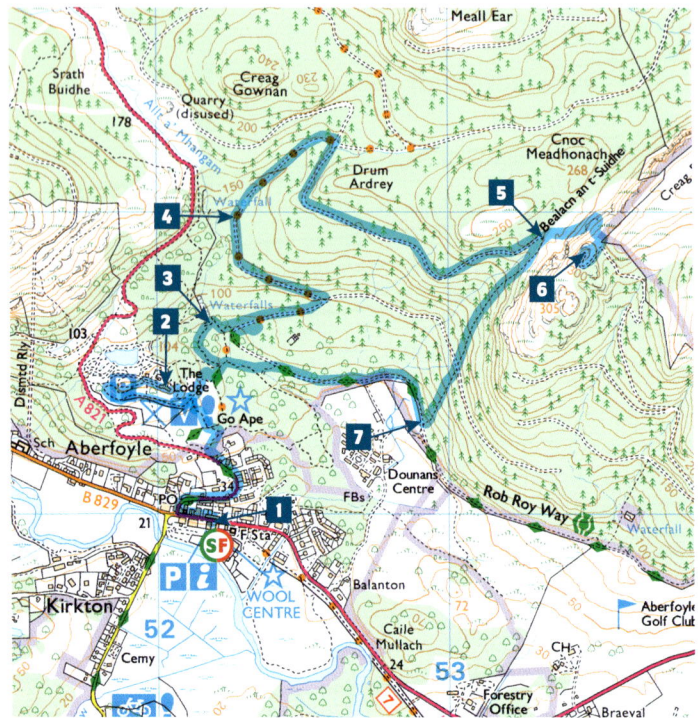

1 From Aberfoyle iCentre, turn left then left again onto Main Street, walk down as far as the Co-op and then turn right, walking up the pavement of the A821 following a sign for 'Trossachs Trail Forest Park Visitor Centre'. Follow the road up through houses for 400m until the pavement runs out. Shortly afterwards, there are some stone steps on the right – take these, then follow signs for **The Lodge** along a steep, well-made path.

Nestled in the forest, The Lodge has a visitor information centre, wildlife webcams and maps. It's a good idea to stop in and speak to their helpful staff to check for updates and current advice – shorter waymarked routes are also available.

2 Facing the entrance of The Lodge, walk around its right-hand side and down a shortcut to the main path.

WALK 14 – LITTLE FAWN WATERFALL AND LIME CRAIG

Turn left onto the main path and begin to follow red markers. When you reach two metal deer sculptures, turn left, then pass some interesting, mirrored human silhouettes. After 200m, pretty **Little Fawn Waterfall** is on your left.

3 Walk over the footbridge here and come to a junction. The main route is straight ahead, but take a short detour to a wildlife hide (ahead and right, marked with a binoculars sign). Red squirrels are frequent visitors to this hide and, sitting quietly, you usually only need to wait a few minutes to see one. From the wildlife hide, return to the junction and turn sharp right, following a red marker to walk away from the river uphill. After 340m, turn left at a junction, following red markers and signs for the N.7 cycle route. Follow this track uphill for 470m to a second, 'secret' **waterfall** and bench.

4 Continue along the track uphill for a further 470m until you reach a crossroads. Here, turn sharp right (south-west) and momentarily downhill, following a red waymarker and sign for 'Lime Craig Trail'. Walk along this track for 1.15km as it levels out for a while before climbing again through a mixture of young and towering coniferous trees – pass a viewpoint and information board about the Highland Boundary Fault, which you are standing on. From this elevated position, you overlook a contrasting Lowland landscape of farmland below.

Deer sculptures near The Lodge

Little Fawn Waterfall

WALK 14 – LITTLE FAWN WATERFALL AND LIME CRAIG

Eventually, you will come to a clearing encircled by boulders at **Beallach an t-Suidhe**, with the overgrown, rocky cliff of Lime Craig Quarry up above.

> This disused limestone quarry is a designated Site of Special Scientific Interest due to its unique geology. Fossils – including trilobites, brachiopods, ostracods – help to date the rock strata of the Highland Boundary Fault and show its links with Scandinavia and North America.

5 The onward route goes off to the right, following red markers, but (if you have the energy) take a narrower path uphill straight ahead, following a 'Path to viewpoint' sign – it's steep with some loose stones, rising above the treeline. When you reach the top, after 300m, turn right onto a narrow, steep path which leads up to a small mast and a viewpoint bench at 311m with a great perspective over the hills to the east.

6 Retrace your steps down to the clearing under Lime Craig and turn left. Follow a waymarked path steeply

Red squirrels at The Lodge's wildlife hide (Photo: Forestry and Land Scotland)

Admiring the view from the Highland Boundary Fault above Lime Craig

downhill as it runs along the course of a small stream below. **There is soon a great view over Aberfoyle and Craigmore.** After 500m, the path is bisected by a wider track – cross this and continue downhill for a further 240m, emerging at a T-junction.

7 Turn right and follow this track for 700m, then take an indicated side path on the left down to a bridge. Cross the bridge and at a fork take the path straight ahead, bearing slightly right towards a waymarker, then turn right onto a larger path that rises uphill through oak trees beside the river. When you reach a junction, turn left, soon passing some round-doored playhouses for children. At the next junction, turn right, then when you reach the deer sculptures, turn left. From this path, turn left onto a path marked for Aberfoyle and follow signs for Aberfoyle downhill back to the road (or continue straight and follow signs for The Lodge).

– To shorten

Avoiding the climb to the viewpoint bench will save 700m walk and 60m of ascent/descent. Turn right at Waypoint 5 instead and follow the waymarked path steeply downhill towards Waypoint 7. Alternatively, you can return the way you've come from Waypoint 5 for a longer, but more gentle descent.

WALK 15
Loch Ard and Lochan a' Ghleannain

Time 2½hr
Distance 7km (4¼ miles)
Climb 120m

A gentle, waymarked, forest route visiting the attractive shorelines of Loch Ard and Lochan a' Ghleannain

Start/finish	Loch Ard Forest car park
Locate	///wizards.wired.captions
Cafes/pubs	None on route
Transport	No public transport
Parking	Loch Ard Forest car park (FK8 3TG)
Toilets	No public toilets on route

Also known as Loch Ard Sculpture Trail, this walk follows waymarked tracks through the mixed woodland of Loch Ard Forest. The route looks out to picturesque islets from the northern shore of tiny Lochan a' Ghleannain, before skirting around the wooded hillock of Creag Bhreac to the south-eastern end of Loch Ard. If you omit the section round the headland, these firm gravel tracks also make for a great family-friendly cycle ride.

Lochan a' Ghleannain

SHORT WALKS TROSSACHS

1 Exit the main car park towards the road. Walk straight ahead at a crossroads (the car exit to the road should be on your right), follow a sign for 'Statute Labour Road Loch Ard' and note a wooden pillar marked with red for 'Loch Ard Sculpture Trail' – this is the route to follow. Pass an overflow car park on your left and continue along a substantial track through mixed woodland as it trends uphill with tall trees on either side. Keep to the main track, ignoring one right-hand and one left-hand turn, for 1.3km to reach a bench at the eastern end of **Lochan a' Ghleannain**.

'Eagle Pole' by sculptor and environmental artist Rob Mulholland

Taking a break beside Loch Ard

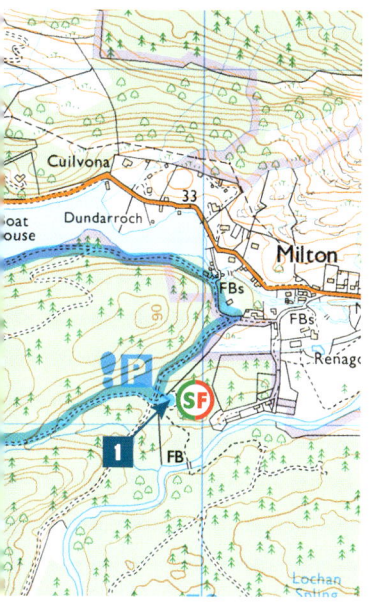

2 Continue along the track with the lochan on your left and the higher ground of **Creag Bhreac** on your right, soon passing a wire sculpture of a flying bird and two tiny, wooded islets in the lochan. Follow the track past the lochan and continue for 500m as it bears round to the right.

3 When the view opens up to Beinn an Fhògharaidh, a hill on the northern side of Loch Ard, look out for a sharp turn to the right – take this, following a red marker through a forest gate, onto another track. Follow this track for 170m, then turn left at the next junction, heading downhill. After a further 460m, as **Loch Ard** comes into view at a T-junction, turn right between a couple of old oaks.

Picturesque houses dotted along the shoreline approaching Lochend

4 Walk along this track for 280m to the next junction, then turn left onto a path that will take you around a headland jutting into the loch.

> In his novel *Rob Roy*, Sir Walter Scott described Loch Ard as an 'enchanting sheet of water'. Rob Roy himself is said to have hidden in a cave near this headland's north-east corner, but its location is far from obvious.

The path becomes narrower, descending left to shore level and a great viewpoint with a bench looking over the loch. Continue along it, with the loch on your left, looking across to idyllically located houses on the northern shore. When you finally reach a junction with the main path, turn left.

5 Pass a picnic bench, continuing with Loch Ard still on your left until the track leaves the shore behind at **The Narrows**, soon passing the mirrored

sculpture, 'Eagle Pole'. Continue along the track as it rejoins the shoreline, pass a forest gate and go straight on at a junction approaching Lochend. Here there is a boathouse and a few houses around the outlet of the loch. Ignore a bridge on your left and keep ahead as the track bends round to the right, passing a gate. When you reach a road junction, turn right, then follow signs for the car park for the last stretch, finally turning left at the crossroads where the walk began.

— To shorten

Instead of going round the headland at Waypoint 4, continue straight along the track and pick up the instructions again at Waypoint 5. This gives a walk of 2hr, 6km and 105m elevation, which keeps to tracks rather than narrower paths.

USEFUL INFORMATION

Tourism bodies

Loch Lomond & The Trossachs National Park www.lochlomond-trossachs.org

Visit Callander www.visitcallander.uk

Visit Scotland www.visitscotland.com

Tourist information centres

Aberfoyle iCentre www.visitscotland.com/info/services/aberfoyle-icentre-p234571

Callander Visitor Information Centre www.visitcallander.uk

The Lodge Forest Visitor Centre https://forestryandland.gov.scot

Travel

Buses

Midland Bluebird (www.mcgillsscotlandeast.co.uk) run the X10A bus service from Glasgow or Stirling to Aberfoyle, and the 59 bus service from Stirling to Callander.

Number 978 Scottish Citylink coaches between Edinburgh and Fort William stop at Callander. Check www.traveline.info for current service providers, routes and times.

The summer-only Trossachs Explorer (www.lochlomond-trossachs.org/the-trossachs-explorer), currently a pilot service, runs between Callander, Kilmahog/Ben Ledi, Brig o' Turk, Ben A'an, Loch Katrine, Ben Venue, The Lodge and Aberfoyle.

USEFUL INFORMATION

Cycles

There is bike hire in Aberfoyle (https://aberfoylebikehire.co.uk), 2.5km south-west of Callander (www.wheelscyclingcentre.com), and at Loch Katherine (www.katrinewheelz.co.uk).

Camping

There are several private campsites in the area, with different facilities for campervans and tents, as well as a basic tent-only site run by the national park at Loch Achray. Visitors planning to wild camp should be aware that Camping Management Zones cover much of the loch- and roadside Trossachs. These bylaws mean a permit is required for tents and campervans, with specific sites set aside for the purpose. Further information: www.lochlomond-trossachs.org/things-to-do/camping.

© Katie Featherstone 2025
First edition 2025
ISBN: 978 1 78631 234 1
eISBN: 978 1 78765 156 2

Printed in Singapore by KHL Printing on responsibly sourced paper.
A catalogue record for this book is available from the British Library.
All photographs are by the author unless otherwise stated.
Cover illustration of Ben A'an by Clare Crooke.

© Crown copyright and database rights 2025 OS AC0000810376

CICERONE

Cicerone Press, Juniper House, Murley Moss, Oxenholme Road, Kendal, Cumbria, LA9 7RL

www.cicerone.co.uk

Updates to this Guide

While every effort is made to ensure the accuracy of guidebooks as they go to print, changes can occur during the lifetime of an edition. Any updates that we know of for this guide will be on the Cicerone website (www.cicerone.co.uk/1234/updates), so please check before planning your trip. We also advise that you check information about transport, accommodation and shops locally. Even rights of way can be altered over time. We are always grateful for information about any discrepancies between a guidebook and the facts on the ground, sent by email to updates@cicerone.co.uk.

Register your book: To sign up to receive free updates, special offers and GPX files where available, create a Cicerone account and register your purchase via the 'My Account' tab at www.cicerone.co.uk.